I am very pleased to be able to offer to you this book, THE ANSWER TO LIFE, by Paul Little, a dear friend who now is in the presence of the Lord he loved.

Paul knew what life is about and had a great ability to present and defend the Christian faith, as these pages show. This book is for you, with my deepest thanks for your prayers and gifts.

BILLY GRAHAM
EVANGELISTIC ASSOCIATION
Minneapolis, Minnesota 55440

THE ANSWER TO LIFE

Paul Little

Foreword by Billy Graham

A new, revised edition
originally published under the title
FAITH IS FOR PEOPLE

CROSSWAY BOOKS • WESTCHESTER, ILLINOIS
A DIVISION OF GOOD NEWS PUBLISHERS

Scripture quotations in this book are taken from the *Revised Standard Version* of the Bible, copyright © 1946, 1952, 1973 by the Division of Christian Education, National Council of Churches of Christ in the U.S.A. Used by permission.

The Answer to Life. Revised edition, copyright © 1987 by Marie Little. Published by Crossway Books, a division of Good News Publishers, Westchester, Illinois 60153.

Original edition copyright © 1976 by Vision House Publishers, under the title *Faith Is For People.*

First printing, revised edition, 1987

Printed in the United States of America

Library of Congress Catalog Card Number 86-72378

ISBN 0-89107-429-5

CONTENTS

Foreword vii

Introduction ix

1   Planet in Crisis 13

2   A Realistic Diagnosis 21

3   A Realistic Solution 29

4   Not a Path But a Person 39

5   Faith Needs an Object 49

6   Is the Object Valid? 57

7   Christ's Credentials 63

8   How Real Is Heaven? 73

9   Can We Be Sure of Heaven? 81

FOREWORD

God has brought me in touch with certain men of outstanding talent. One such was my friend the late Paul Little whom I first came to appreciate in a special way in 1957 when he tirelessly reached out to university students in our sixteen-week New York Crusade. I have deeply admired him as a man of God, with extraordinary insights into the work of God and boundless enthusiasm for communicating the Word of God.

I sense a great personal loss because Paul is no longer with us and feel privileged to recommend this stimulating series of talks which he gave at The Village Church I once pastored in suburban Chicago.

In his unique way Paul describes "the electricity of Christ's claim" that He is the solution to the "moral power failure" of our time. Then he shows how Jesus Christ speaks to us today as clearly as He did to the thief on the cross, "You, too, can be with me in Paradise."

Maybe you have stood on the perimeter of Christianity and questioned what it is all about. Is it really true? Does it have any pertinence to my life? What happens if I ignore it? Or perhaps you have been discouraged in the past by some ponderous, cliché-ridden explanations. This book, then, is for you. You will find here an authenticity that comes from a man who was unconditionally devoted to Jesus Christ.

Billy Graham

INTRODUCTION

The sprawling auditorium of the Village Church in Western Springs (IL) vibrated with the hum of voices as the opening hour of 7 P.M. drew near. Cultured, sophisticated, self-assured suburbanites gathered for the Friday night meeting. It was the first of four Friday nights in a lecture series to define the Christian faith for the adult beginner. Neighbors and friends had come with church members.

At 7 my husband, Paul Little, began his talk with a question, "Why would three affluent teenagers murder an innocent man?" Paul went on to discuss the world's search for answers to this and other dilemmas. He examined diagnoses and solutions people have proposed. Then he took the audience back to the diagnosis and solution advanced by Jesus two thousand years ago and still relevant today.

Paul's ability to present the vital aspects of Christianity to the unchurched and to mix in meaningful illustrations sprang from his twenty-seven years of lecturing to college and university students on five continents. He never shrank from "getting into the ring" to uphold the credibility of the Christian faith. It was his custom to say that there was no argument anyone could pose that would suddenly bring the whole of Christianity crashing into ruins.

Paul was only forty-seven when his earthly ministry abruptly ended in a head-on collision. I am personally grateful for the cassettes containing some of his most powerful messages accompanied by the music of his voice, but I am even more grateful that the enduring quality of the truths he communicated so clearly can be preserved.

Marie H. Little

1 PLANET IN CRISIS

Why would three affluent teenagers murder an innocent man?

The whole nation was shocked at the story of how these young people under the influence of drugs brutally beat and killed a man. Then we began to realize once more that murder and drugs are symptoms of the malignant disease spreading throughout our society.

Secular leaders of society as well as religious leaders are decrying this disease. The senior editor of a secular magazine wrote, "Most Americans hate to admit we are in a crisis, but its bitter fruits are all around us—the racist, the wild kid, the price-rigging executive, the pregnant high school girl, the dope addict, the bribed athlete, the un-cared-for aged, the poor, the criminal.

The problem isn't only in the United States. Thoughtful people all over the world realize that we're facing a tremendous worldwide crisis. Among other things, the advent of nuclear weapons has radically changed life's outlook for everybody. The late President Kennedy observed that mankind faced its greatest crisis in history.

Where Have We Gone Wrong?

While everyone knows that something is wrong with the world, people don't agree on the cause of the problem. What is it that makes us victims of a haunting fear? What is it that plagues this age of unprecedented technological progress? Whatever our point of view, I think we all would agree that before we can ever arrive at a workable solution to any problem, we first need to come up with an accurate diagnosis. Bona-fide cures are always directly related to accurate diagnoses.

If I had a stomachache and somebody diagnosed me as having indigestion and gave me Pepto-Bismol, whereas I had acute appendicitis, I could be in pretty grim shape by morning! If the cure isn't based on an accurate diagnosis, it's a worthless cure. On the other hand, if all I had was indigestion and some eager surgeon took my appendix out, that wouldn't be helpful either! It might relieve me from possible problems later on, but it wouldn't be the solution to my immediate problem, which could have been taken care of with Pepto-Bismol. Diagnosis and cure go hand in hand.

It's interesting to notice that since the beginning of the twentieth century three major diagnoses of the world's problems have been advanced, along with corollary solutions, by thinkers of our time.

Education As a Cure

One diagnosis, widely held before World War II, is ignorance. The solution to this, proponents said, could be achieved by universal education. H. G. Wells, the noted British philosopher and historian, was one of the most vocal adherents of this view. According to this view, man is basically good and all that is required to fully perfect him is to educate him.

We all want as much education as we can get, but on closer analysis it would seem that this diagnosis is rather inadequate. As a matter of fact, Mr. Wells himself later abandoned his point of view. World War I came as a shock to him as he saw nations becoming involved in an incredible holocaust. But he and many others at the time explained this slaughter as "the war to end all wars." They suggested that man had slipped on the ladder of progress, but was finally ready to complete the program begun before being slowed by World War I.

When only twenty years later World War II came along and buried World War I by comparison, it was becoming obvious that some of the most highly educated nations in the world were participating in the most incredible atrocities that mankind had ever known. After the reality of World War II H. G. Wells wrote a book called

Mind at the End of Its Tether, in which he concluded that "man is not worth educating." The historical fact of World War II had completely shattered his optimistic opinion that human nature could be perfected. While Wells still believed in education for certain purposes, he recognized that the problem of human nature required more than mere education.

Knowledge Is Not Virtue

Many philosophers abandoned Wells' position even though they had been proponents of it prior to World War II, and pessimism now became the vogue in philosophical circles. This is probably best exemplified by Jean-Paul Sartre, the Nobel Prize winner, in his existentialist philosophy.

Education can be useful, but if education were the solution to the human problem, we could expect to find that the university community (since it presumably has the greatest corner on knowledge and information) would be the most moral segment of any society.

In my visits to hundreds of university campuses all over the United States and in other countries I would have to say, as much as I would like to think otherwise, that the university community is not the moral apex in any given society. In fact, it's often far from the top in that respect. Scandals at military academies and universities show that education in itself does not guarantee moral behavior.

Man's problem is not *knowing* what he ought to do. It is to *do* what he knows to be right. Everyone throughout the world agrees that war is wrong, but that doesn't stop war. Knowledge is not virtue in this sense. Knowledge is useful, but a problem lies beyond it.

C. S. Lewis, the late English author, was closer to the truth when he made the rather cryptic observation that education, as useful as it is, seems only to serve to make man a more clever devil. Education in itself doesn't solve the basic moral dilemma of the human race.

Others say poverty is the basic problem of the world. According to this thesis, everything is determined by economics, and the solution to the world's problem is essentially economic equality. We recognize this as a basic tenet of dialectical Marxism.

All will agree that every human being should have enough food to eat, adequate clothing, housing, and medical care, and that we should work to make this possible for people. Yet on closer analysis, as appealing as this diagnosis and solution sound, it is a superficial analysis of the human problem. The United States bears eloquent testimony to the fact that economic prosperity is an inadequate diagnosis for the human dilemma.

The United States leads the world in economic standards. We have the greatest number of telephones, bathtubs, automobiles, and television sets, and the highest per capita income in the world, but we also lead the world in crime, juvenile delinquency, and divorce. It seems that economic affluence does not solve the primary problem of the human race and human nature. If we happen to know people with lots of money, we realize that many of them bear testimony to the fact that, as useful as money is and as much as we would all like to have more of it than we do, money in itself does not bring satisfaction to the people who have it.

The Anguish of Affluence

People were surprised by the apparent suicide of an heir to a corporate fortune. One of his friends reported that he had said shortly before his suicide that life had no meaning for him because he had so much money.

For many people in the world today, money represents all of life's meaning to them. They give all of their energy to accumulating money. Then they find it doesn't satisfy their inner longing. As useful as money is (none of us would turn down a legacy), economic affluence does not solve the deep-seated problem of the world.

The secular analysis of this is found in a careful study by two New York psychiatrists. Their book, *The Split-Level Trap*, describes residents of a suburban county in northern New Jersey—people who achieved more economic affluence than they had anticipated and as a result were unhappy in their personal lives. Though many of these people had looked to money as a source of satisfaction, meaning and purpose in life, they found that this was not the case, and disillusionment set in despite achievement of the economic goals toward which they had worked so hard. So economic success fails to get at the root of the problem.

Science to the Rescue?

A third diagnosis of the world's problems is technological lag. This means the lag in applying scientific methods to social and human problems. In this view, technological advance offers the basic solution. This thesis notes that we have made tremendous strides through science (and of course we have, and all of us are grateful for the fruits of scientific research and dazzled by the space age in which we live), but because we have devoted much of our technological energies to defense, we have missed getting on top of social problems by not applying the scientific method to them. Adherents say that if only we would do this we would begin to find the way out of our dilemmas.

Thoughtful observers (including some of the leading scientists of our day), however, are beginning to recognize that, as tremendously useful as the scientific method is as a gateway to discovery, and as tremendously blessed as we have been by the fruits of research and endeavor, nothing in the scientific method itself is capable of giving moral direction. Nothing within the scientific method itself will decide whether the fruits of nuclear research are used to destroy cities or to destroy cancer. This is a moral problem which lies beyond science. It is a problem within ourselves.

We don't really fear nuclear weapons. We fear the men who have them. In the hands of someone who is honest, just, loving, and kind, nuclear weapons are as harmless as a baby's rattle. In the hands of unscrupulous persons who would do anything to achieve power, they can become instruments of world annihilation."

Erich Fromm, the renowned psychiatrist, observed, "Technologically we're in the space age, emotionally we're in the stone age." Even scientists recognize that more than science is needed. The late Dr. Carl Compton, a prominent nuclear physicist, warned, "Unless the human race experiences and achieves a moral and spiritual advance equal to the technological advance that it has made, we are on the verge of annihilation."

If you've been thinking through these solutions, you may have noted that all have one common characteristic—they are external to people. Universal education is outside a person; economic equality and technological research are too. People don't want to take the blame for the mess that the world is in!

2 A REALISTIC DIAGNOSIS

The one diagnosis of the world's problems that appears to be most akin to human experience and most realistic in terms of history was advanced almost two thousand years ago by Jesus of Nazareth in a conversation with a group of religious leaders called Pharisees. As men who had externalized the human problem and its solution, they were very concerned with all kinds of ceremonial rules such as how they washed their hands or didn't wash them before they ate and what utensils they used. Jesus told them they had missed the point by externalizing the problem.

That conversation is recorded in the Gospel of Mark. "He called the people to him again and said to them, 'Hear me, all of you, and understand: there is nothing outside a man which by going into him can defile him; but the things which come out of a man are what defile him.' And when he had entered the house and left the people, his disciples asked him about the parable. And he said to them, 'Then are you also without understanding? Do you not see that whatever goes into a man from outside cannot defile him, since it enters not his heart but his stomach, and so passes on?'" (Mark 7:14-19).

It's Not What We Eat

Thus Jesus declared all foods clean and went on to give examples of what comes out of people's hearts. He named fornication, theft, murder, adultery, coveting, wickedness, deceit, licentiousness, envy, slander, pride, and foolishness. All these evils come *from within*, and it is these that defile a man. He told them they had missed the point completely. The basic problem of the human race is *internal*. Our personal problems come from within us, and this defilement has separated us from God our Maker.

It's interesting to note that Jesus discussed thoughts and actions in almost the same breath. He spoke of murder and hatred and impurity of thought, which indicates thoughts as well as actions are evidence of man's basic problem. God considers our *attitudes* as well as our actions. The fact is that some of us have never done certain things that other people have done (who we look down upon and think ourselves superior to) simply because we have not been tempted in the same way. Yet if our thought life were to be exposed, if we were to be known as we really are inside, we would find ourselves in the same situation as other people: separated from God because of defilement.

God Is Holy

We know from other teachings of Jesus that because God is absolutely pure and holy we cannot exist in His presence if we are defiled. *This* is the basic problem of the human race—separation from the God who created us. We as the human race and we as individuals are separated from God by our sins.

Author E. Stanley Jones sent his book on conversion to Carl Gustav Jung. Jones wondered what kind of response he would get from the famous European psychiatrist, because generally speaking many psychiatrists have not been too sympathetic to a supernatural or religious point of view. Jones was astounded when he received a letter from Jung saying, "Those psychiatrists who are not superficial have come to the conclusion that the vast neurotic misery of the world could be termed a neurosis of emptiness. Men cut themselves from the root of their being, from God, and then life turns empty, inane, meaningless, without purpose, so when God goes, goal goes, when goal goes, meaning goes, when meaning goes, value goes, and life turns dead on our hands." That's an interesting echo of the diagnosis that Jesus advanced two thousand years ago as the basic problem of the human race.

It's Called Sin

Jesus called the internal condition which causes human problems *sin*. In our society today the word *sin* does not communicate very well. People usually associate sin with immorality, and if they don't happen to be immoral, they get highly incensed because they think the word doesn't apply to them.

Immorality is only one aspect of sin, which is a disease of the human race. Though it is universal, the symptoms vary from person to person. Every culture and every stratum of society holds a self-centered and rebellious or indifferent attitude toward God, the Creator. It is interesting to note that the basic root of each sin Jesus mentioned is essentially self-centeredness.

The Big I

Basically, our problems in society are the result of self-centeredness carried to communal, national, and international levels. Whether its two people who can't get along in a home, community tension, or nations in conflict self-centeredness prevails in our relationships because we have become separated from God and rebelled against Him.

God created us to function in a way that would bring us the greatest happiness and meaning. He intended for us to have a close relationship with Himself—one which in turn would affect our relationship with others. Instead we are somewhat like an automobile which is constructed to function only when there is an intelligent, sober driver behind the wheel, but if shoved off a hill without a driver careens down the hill, wreaking damage along the way and crashing.

The first man rebelled against God and, so to speak, shoved God out of the driver's seat of his life. In a sense every one of us has ratified that decision, thereby causing our problem. We're like lamps unplugged from sockets. We are cut off from the source of moral power, from the dynamics that God intends us to have.

Other results of this separation are emptiness, meaninglessness, frustration, and loneliness. This is the "lonely crowd" idea that David Riesman, a Harvard sociologist, wrote about in his book.

Another result is guilt. We find ourselves unable to shake off a guilt that is ours because of deliberate wrongdoing somewhere along the line. We have a lack of self-control; we grind our gears, wishing we could change our behavior patterns. We vow over and over that we will change, but we find that we are unable to change even though we want to very much.

Better Is Not Perfect

You may be wondering, Do you mean to say that all of us are as bad as the three teenage murderers? No, that's obviously not the case. There is a vast difference in the quality of lives that people live. Some live far better lives than others, but still can't meet the eternal God's standard of infinite holiness and perfection. Because of God's perfect character, the only way we can be in dynamic relationship with Him is to be perfect ourselves. Measured against that standard, every one of us has failed. We may be better than someone else, but unless we have absolute perfection we cannot make it in the terms that God has laid down and in the light of His own character.

A commercial airliner crashed into a mountaintop while trying to land at Las Vegas in a snowstorm. The most tragic thing about the crash was that it occurred only a couple of feet from the top of the mountain. Another few feet and the plane would have made it over the mountain, but all of those people were as dead as if they had crashed a thousand feet farther down.

Though there are differences in morality, absolute perfection is necessary in God's sight.

Think of Hawaii as representing God's standard of holiness and righteousness. Then imagine lining up the whole human race on the west coast of California and saying each person must swim to Hawaii. Everyone's success or failure will be determined by the moral quality of the life he lives. Here is a very upstanding person in the community, yet one who would be the first to admit that he is imperfect. (The interesting thing is that the better a person is, the more conscious he is of his own failure!) You've probably noticed this as one of the characteristics of a good person. Here he is seventy-five miles out and still churning. Then there are the Joe College types, just happy-go-lucky people not really bad enough for Alcatraz. They get smashed on the weekends and cheat on a few exams, but they're not ready for federal prison yet. They are, let's say, ten miles out. And then there are the derelicts from skid row, only five hundred yards offshore but practically drowning.

There's no comparison in the quality of lives that these people have lived, is there? There's a big difference between them. Yet in terms of the ultimate objective, Hawaii, they're all in exactly the same situation—far short of the goal. The only way any of them is going to make it to Hawaii is with the help of a ship or plane. No one can do it alone.

This is essentially what Jesus Christ said about our life situation—the human race is suffering from a mortal disease which He calls sin and which separates us from God.

What's wrong with the world? G. K. Chesterton answered accurately for all of us: "*I'm* wrong with the world."

Jesus not only diagnosed the problem which separates us from God, but He gave us the dynamic solution.

Jesus said He is the solution. "I came that they might have life, and have it abundantly" (John 10:10).

He went on to explain that the reason He had come into human history was not only to tell us what God was like, but to make it possible for us to be forgiven and given new life that would bring us into a vital relationship with God.

Someone has said that the vice president of the United States is "only a heartbeat away from the presidency." We are only a prayer away from a dynamic relationship with the living God, our Creator. Yet many in the world do not recognize Him as the solution.

3 A REALISTIC SOLUTION

In a survey, schoolchildren in a large city were asked, "Do you believe that God understands nuclear energy?" *Sixty-four percent of them replied no!* To their young minds God had been left in the dust of scientific progress. In terms of modern living, many people see God and the church as totally irrelevant.

After presenting the gospel at Queens University in Kingston, Ontario, we opened the floor for discussion. A bearded graduate student took a pipe out of his mouth and looked at me in a pitying way as he asked, "Why do you Christians bother?" The impact of what he said went far beyond his words, and his attitude typified that of many people. "What does your message have to do with life itself?"

One of the best ways to answer this allegation of irrelevance is to ask ourselves what characterizes modern man and to show how the Lord Jesus Christ speaks to man's needs in this twentieth-century space age. We hear about "modern man come of age." Dietrich Bonhoeffer popularized the expression "man come of age" as a person who has outgrown his need of God, at least in the traditional Christian concept. Let's examine modern man to see if this is true.

The Lonely Crowd

One of the major characteristics of our time is loneliness. It is ironic that in this age of the greatest population explosion the world has ever known, when there are more bodies per square foot than there have ever been, more people are desperately lonely. Many factors contribute to this loneliness. For one thing, we are a rootless, mobile society in which people often don't live and die near relatives or have their support.

Many people are caught in lonely affluence. Even though they have an abundance of material things, they are cut off from the society around them. We are a depersonalized society despite a population explosion.

I experienced a frightening example of depersonalization. Month after month I kept getting a bill for $165 from an oil company, because the computer had run amok or suffered a headache. I called twice and wrote three letters, but I continued to receive the computerized bill, the one that says, "Do not fold, spindle, or mutilate." Finally I crumpled it into a ball and mailed it in an envelope with a note that said, "Dear Sir: Perhaps this will get me some personal attention." And it did. The next month I got my regular bill.

There is suburban loneliness and there is urban loneliness. The high-rise apartments that we see in urban neighborhoods are monuments to loneliness. I personally know of more than one person, both in the cities and in the suburbs, who goes to the large shopping centers simply for the opportunity of talking to somebody in the stores, if only the supermarket checker. Some people are lonely even within their families.

The Good Shepherd

Jesus responded to the problem of loneliness with wonderful words: "I am the Good Shepherd; I know my own sheep and my own know me" (John 10:14). When He comes into our experience as Savior and Lord, He is our shepherd and will never leave us or forsake us. He speaks powerfully to this question of loneliness. We need to remind ourselves of this, and to communicate this to a world around us that is desperately lonely.

If we are not careful, we tend to slip into the thinking of a non-Christian age. We know that no personnel manager can personally handle more than fifty people in any way, shape, or form, and since there are almost four billion people on the face of the earth, we wonder how God can possibly be truly concerned about us and our piddling problems. Yet we read that the very hairs of our heads are numbered, that two sparrows don't fall to the ground without the Heavenly Father knowing it.

The Friend of Friends

While we were living in New York a girl from Barnard College came to talk to my wife, Marie. She was a girl who had been deeply hurt, even by her own family, and she had come to the place where she couldn't trust anybody. As my wife told her of the comforting promises of the Lord Jesus Christ, and how He could meet this problem of hurt and loneliness in her life, she said with tears, "You mean to say He'll never leave me?" Christ's assurance of His personal presence is as true as the God of the universe. In my travels I am often in Podunk Junction where I don't know a soul. It's tremendous to realize that I am never alone.

A true friend knows the worst about us but still remains our friend. This is consummately true of our Lord. He knows we aren't prize packages, but He still loves us. He knows us better than we know ourselves.

A doctor who had been a profligate all his life became a Christian through an evangelistic crusade. About a year after his conversion some of his old cronies came to him and said, "When you're away from all your religious friends and their environment and all by yourself, don't you sometimes wish you could get back into the old life with us?" The doctor looked at them and said, "Yes, sometimes I do, but then I realize that I'm never alone. That's what makes the difference."

When we come to the Savior, not only does

Jesus come into our lives and promise to be our constant companion and a friend who sticks closer than a brother, but He also ushers us into the most wonderful fellowship in the world, the church of Jesus Christ.

In other countries I've had the experience of meeting someone with whom I could hardly communicate verbally, but with whom there was a tremendous communication of spirit in Christ. In ten minutes I feel closer to a fellow-believer than I do to relatives who don't know the Savior. Despite all its problems, the church, which is also metaphorically called the Body of Christ, meaning believers united by the Holy Spirit to Christ in one body (Rom. 12:5; Eph. 1:22-23), is still the most wonderful group of people this side of heaven.

Comparing the church with secular fellowship, the church stands out even more vividly. I have noticed on campuses that if you are a member of a social fraternity, you are supposed to have a great bond with other members—the secret handshake and so forth. These fraternities show a bond up to a point, but I've been in chapter meetings more than once when a brother from another chapter arrives and is introduced as a member of Psi Delta or whatever. "Let's give Brother Jones a hand," the chapter leader says. Brother Jones is given a hand, a free meal, and a bed for the night, but then he's ignored for the rest of the stay. He's as lonely in a chapter of his own fraternity as he would be in another city hundreds of miles away. He's got a meal and a bed, and that's good, but in terms of vital fellowship, it just isn't there.

When the church of Christ functions the way it should, there is true Christian fellowship instead of superficial fraternal camaraderie. "Now you are the body of Christ and individual members of it" (1 Cor. 12:27).

What Does It All Mean?

More and more secularists are writing about another problem of modern man—the phenomenon of meaninglessness, or lack of purpose in life. We're in this great rat race, working and striving like crazy, but where does it all lead? What does it mean?

If I had to put students on the campuses of North America in one category I would say they lack purpose. They don't know *why* they're studying *what* they're studying apart from the fact that Mom and Dad sent them to college. It's all so meaningless.

This is the whole thesis of existentialism, the philosophy of despair and meaninglessness. Though Shakespeare probably did not think of himself as an existentialist, he was in that league without realizing it when he wrote, "Life is a tale told by an idiot, full of sound and fury, signifying nothing." That's what many people have concluded today.

Jean-Paul Sartre, a French philosopher who won the Nobel Prize for his writings, produced a play called *No Exit*, which espoused essentially the same despair-oriented conclusion that Shakespeare had written centuries earlier. Sartre also wrote a book called *Nausea*, which describes life as Sartre saw it. Albert Camus, the French novelist, wrote of the absurdity of life. Meaning for him is accepting meaninglessness and living on the edge of the abyss, for life itself has no real meaning.

The Light of the World

Is Christianity relevant to this problem of despair which characterizes our age? Does Jesus Christ speak to this problem? He said, "I am the light of the world; he who follows me will not walk in darkness, but will have the light of life" (John 8:12).

Have you ever been in a dark room that was unfamiliar to you? You groped your way around trying to find a light switch, and as you bumped into something your heart beat three times faster. Then something brushed your face and you jumped three feet off the floor. You became what we might call "unzipped"—completely disoriented. You felt completely insecure.

That's the way a lot of people are living life. They're groping desperately, looking for meaning. They're trying this philosophy or that cult, but they're in despair because none is doing for them what they had hoped.

You also know the feeling when you find the switch and the light goes on. Immediately you're oriented. You know how to get where you want to go. That's exactly what Jesus promises to do for us in life. "I am the light of the world; he who follows me will not walk in darkness, but will have the light of life."

To follow Him we first must acknowledge our sin and invite Him into our lives as Savior and Lord. Then He ties our lives into God's purpose, not only for time, but for eternity. This is true purpose! One of the joys of the Christian life is to allow God to show us His plan and purpose. Even the routine chores of life—such as mowing the lawn, changing the diapers, washing the dishes, studying physics, and playing chess—tie in with His purpose, as well as those so-called spiritual aspects of our lives, such as praying, reading the Bible, or witnessing. The *totality* of our lives is given to the Savior for Him to use as He chooses. When we are transformed, we are able to draw on His strength to do *everything* to the glory of God. This is reality when we enter into personal fellowship with the one who is the light of the world. Is Christianity relevant to this modern age that has lost its meaning and purpose, that has lost its way? Yes, it is. The relevancy of Christianity is found in Christ Himself, the only true light of the world.

After the Party

Another problem that characterizes our time is emptiness—a feeling that creeps over a person like a cold fog after the party is over. It's the feeling we get when all of the external stimulations are gone, when the TV or transistor radio goes dead and we can't get it fixed until the next morning when the stores open, and we're shut up to silence, emptiness. We have nothing to draw on from within. Many people are able to exist only because of external stimulation, and they become frightened and disturbed when they're shut up to themselves. Psychiatrist Rollo May describes them as "hollow" people. Beyond the exterior there is nothing. Life has become completely banal. Carl Gustav Jung, the Swiss psychiatrist, said shortly before he died that "the central neurosis of our time is emptiness."

It is remarkable to me that it is the secularists, to a large extent, who are diagnosing society and individual problems in these terms. In this climate Christians have opportunity to share the answer to life in Jesus Christ, because secularists are finally beginning to realize the truth of what the Bible has said for two thousand years.

Better Homes and Boredom

Boredom is a prevalent characteristic of our time. A startling fact is that juvenile delinquency is caused, to a large extent, by boredom. This is why, contrary to earlier predictions, many juvenile delinquents are coming from so-called "better homes" rather than from ghettos or the other side of the tracks. Young people are bored and empty because there is nothing within to sustain them.

Recognition of this fact is coming from remarkable quarters. A novel entitled *Not by Bread Alone* was smuggled out of the Soviet Union. Even in a Communistic society, which is dedicated to the philosophic proposition that only the material is real, many are coming to realize that this philosophy is not true, that there needs to be something beyond the material to sustain the spirit of man.

Jesus, knowing this, said, "I am the bread of life; he who comes to me shall never hunger, and he who believes on me shall never thirst" (John 6:35). As we come into a personal relationship with Jesus Christ and remain in this vital relationship day by day, He sustains us from within. When the disciples were concerned whether He had anything to eat after His conversation with the woman at the well, He answered, "I have meat to eat that you know not of . . . to do the will of him who sent me" (John 4:32-34).

We can share in that spiritual sustenance as we come to know Him and seek to do His will. He sustains us in that dimension of life that can never be satisfied by cramming with material things.

4 NOT A PATH BUT A PERSON

I recall a vivid illustration of Christ versus materialism in Fort Lauderdale. After a day of beach evangelism with college students we went back to the hotel, where we heard the owner of the hotel give his personal testimony. Mr. Charles Pitts of Toronto stood up and told the students that his personal ambition in life had been to make a million dollars by the time he was forty years old. "By the time I was thirty-five I had made my first million, and by the time I was forty I had made six million." This wasn't hard to believe as we looked around at the plush hotel of which Mr. Pitts was the owner!

He related how he had thought that getting things would give satisfaction, but as he acquired more and more things, he found that he was not satisfied. His wife became restless, so he bought her homes in three or four places around the world, trying desperately to satiate her longing, but this didn't work either.

Then Mr. Pitts told the students how his wife began to read the Bible and get comfort from it. He thought this was kind of a nutty thing to do, but if it calmed her, well, any port would do in a storm. He bought a couple of Bibles for her to read. Soon she seemed to undergo a whole change of outlook toward life. She talked about knowing Christ personally, which to him was so much gobbledygook. He didn't understand this religious stuff—he thought it was nonsense, and certainly not for him. Perhaps it was okay for an emotional woman, but not for a hardheaded businessman.

Mr. Pitts related how he increasingly realized that his life was not giving him all that he wanted. At the request of his wife he went reluctantly to an evangelistic meeting, even while his planes were being readied at the airport to take him on his annual hunting trip. He told how that night God the Holy Spirit convicted him of his need and how he came to the Savior. Mr. Pitts closed his testimony by declaring that when we are on the bottom rung of the ladder, the top looks bright and rosy; when we finally get to the top, we find nothing there to satisfy the emptiness we all feel because of separation from God our Maker. Jesus Christ alone can fill that void.

His testimony had a profound impact on the students. It surprised them to learn that becoming a multimillionaire in itself wouldn't satisfy the inner longings of their hearts.

Happiness over the Horizon

If we're not married, we think, "Things aren't too good now, but when we get married, they will be." If we're not making too much money now, we think, "When we get more money coming in, that will do it." Then we get the first job and we think, "It must come after the next promotion." And so it goes on with the first car and the second, and always it's the next thing over the horizon that will satisfy the emptiness.

Jesus said, "I am the bread of life; he who comes to me shall never hunger, and he who believes in me shall never thirst" (John 6:35). The tremendous thing that happens when we come into personal relationship with the Lord Jesus Christ, the thing which we can communicate with confidence and power to our friends, is that we receive life and deep-seated joy that doesn't depend on circumstances.

Most people apart from Christ are tied to circumstances. When they're up, they're up, and when they're down, they're down. But if we really know Christ and are in vital fellowship with Him, we are able to transcend circumstances, whatever they may be. This reality is what enabled Paul to say, "I have learned in whatever state I am, therewith to be content" (Phil. 4:11). He didn't appreciate prisons and scorpions and snakes and rats any more than you or I do, but he had something that went far beyond that to sustain him. It was the reality of Christ that sent the early Christians singing to the den of lions. It was knowing the one who is the bread and water of life.

Christians are not immune to circumstances; the tragedies and sufferings of life have their impact, but we have an inner contentment, an inner peace, that goes far beyond the temporary waves on the surface.

Moral Power Failure

Another problem in society is what I call a moral power failure. We are finding a breakdown in ethical morality at every level of society: in government, in industry, in business, and most certainly on college campuses.

I talk to many who *know* what is right but find themselves *doing*, sometimes continuously, what they would have dreamed they would do. They hate themselves for it afterwards, but find themselves drawn to the same sins again. Secular novelists and playwrights explicitly describe this struggle. It's not even necessary to see the play to know what they are saying. If you read reviews in the news magazines, the dilemma of the person without God is clear.

He Is the Life

Knowing what to do and doing it are not the same. Anyone in a moral dilemma needs more than good advice. If all the Lord did when He came into human history was to give us a Sermon on the Mount, as wonderful and great as that sermon is, He would have only increased our frustration. We've had some kind of golden rule from the earliest dawn of history, from the time of Confucius on down. But our Lord did far more than this; He said, "I am the life" and "I came that they might have life, and have it more abundantly" (John 14:6; 10:10).

As I have studied non-Christian religions, I have been impressed again and again with the uniqueness of the Lord Jesus Christ. Every other religious leader of the world says essentially, "This is the way; if you take this way and succeed, you will make it at the end." The problem is, of course, that nobody can make it.

Jesus doesn't give a set of swimming instructions to a drowning man. He says, "I am the way. You come to Me and I will give you My life." He releases this life in us so that we are able to live in the reality and the power which He offers us. The reason the Christian is able to live a life that is supernatural is because the life that he has in the Lord Jesus Christ is supernatural. How is it possible to love somebody who is inherently unlovely? It's not possible by pumping ourselves up and saying, "I ought to love him. I ought to love him. I am going to think positively and come to this." No. It is because the Lord Jesus Christ comes into our lives as the one who is the life.

Someone has suggested, and I think aptly, that the Christian life is not so much a *path* as it is a *person*. Christ is our life, and we look to Him day by day. In all the circumstances of life in which we don't have the power to do what we know we should do, we find our Lord coming to us and releasing His power into our lives.

Everybody knows that war is wrong, but knowledge doesn't change war or stop war. We need a power which is strong enough to make a liar tell the truth, to make a profligate pure, to make a thief honest. We need a power that can break the chain of drug addiction, that can break the prison of alcoholism, that can make all of us holy people in God's sight.

This power is Jesus Christ Himself. "I am the life," He says. Not His teaching, which is important, but He *personally* is the life. The dynamic of Christianity is the fact that the Lord Jesus Christ is a living person who can enter into the life of any person who invites Him. You and I are able to live in the reality of this relationship today because Christ is not just a good idea; He is a personality. "I am come that they might have life more abundantly." Does our Lord speak to the problem of moral power failure? Powerfully. He is the only one who can help us when we cannot help ourselves.

The Problem of Guilt

Another problem people are trying to deal with is guilt. Secularists are commenting on this too; and increasingly they are coming to realize that there is a distinction between guilt and a guilt complex. A guilt complex is feeling very guilty about something for which there is no rational basis for guilt. On the other hand, guilt is an absolutely normative part of human personality, as Dr. O. Hobart Mowrer of the University of Illinois points out in his book *The Crisis in Psychiatry and Religion*. If you stab your mother to death and feel no guilt about it, there is something tragically abnormal about you.

At Queens University in Kingston a man got into our discussion and told how, a year before, he had come to know the Lord Jesus Christ through Dr. Fred Smith of the University of Minnesota. The man said, "My life was so racked up that I didn't know which way to turn. I was so corrupt from within that I needed a bath from the inside out. When I came to know Christ, I got that bath. I just can't describe the difference to you. For twenty-four hours after this happened to me I just sat thinking about its implication, it was so profound in its impact on me."

Does Jesus speak to our gnawing guilt? He says, "I am the door; if any one enters by me he shall be saved, and will go in and out and find pasture" (John 10:9). Paul alludes to this same forgiveness: "He [God] made him [Jesus Christ] to be sin, who knew no sin, so that in him we might become the righteousness of God" (2 Cor. 5:21). When we come to the Savior as the door to heaven we are saved; we experience forgiveness and cleansing from within. This is a tremendous reality to a world that feels the guilt of sin and desperately wants forgiveness and cleansing.

Restlessness

Another problem we have today is restlessness. The phenomenal sale of books on peace of mind and soul, and variations on that theme, indicates that these authors have touched something that is on the minds of many people today. If you speak on the subject of inner peace today, you inevitably attract a crowd, because most people have no inner peace.

A doctor friend on the West Coast took an informal poll over a period of three years. He asked his patients, "If you had one desire that you knew would be granted without any question, what would you ask?" Eighty-seven percent of the respondents said they would ask for peace of mind and soul!

In a discussion with a number of scientists from around the world, a presentation of the gospel was made, and a discussion of Christianity followed. One very brilliant man, a Ph.D., said, "I don't see this Christianity business. I've got everything you Christians have. I've got a lovely home, I love my wife, I'm kind to my neighbor, and I pay my bills." But then he paused for a moment and added, "The only thing is, I can't sleep at night."

We began to discuss how the Lord Jesus Christ could meet his problem of inner turmoil, and I believe he's now on the way to the kingdom. Jesus said, "Peace I leave with you; my peace I give unto you. Not as the world gives do I give unto you. Let not your heart be troubled, neither let it be afraid" (John 14:27). "Come unto me, all you who labor and are heavily laden, and I will give you rest" (Matt. 11:28). Rest and peace are the kind of words we want to savor, as we would a favorite candy. They are comforting. This comfort we can have through Jesus Christ, who speaks with such

powerful relevance to the problem of inner turmoil today.

Fear of Death

Anxiety is another problem secularists are recog-
nizing as a grave one. Fear of the future and fear
of death grip many of us—not when we're sitting
in a nice warm room with friends, but when we're
facing surgery and other crises. Sooner or later
death becomes very real to us. Jesus spoke to this
fear when He said, "I am the resurrection and the
life; he who believes in me, though he die, yet
shall he live, and whoever lives and believes in me
shall never die" (John 11:25, 26). *He* delivers us
from fear of the future, because we know our
lives are in His hand, that nothing happens by
accident, and that death takes us into the presence of God for eternity.

I used to wonder whether Christ could really
give peace at a time of death. One of the by-
products of my heart surgery was that I proved in
my own life that the peace of Christ is real. I had
always *said* it was real, but it's exciting to experience it! I'll never forget the tremendous peace
that came into my heart and soul as I was wheeled
into that operating room. I knew this peace was
not from myself. Though I thought I would
probably survive the surgery, I also knew that
there was a possibility I wouldn't. A heart oper-
ation can be a technical success and the patient
still die because one of seventy-three other things

went wrong! Jesus as *the* life speaks with powerful relevance to our fear of death.

"I Am the Truth"

Jesus also said, "I am the truth" (John 14:6). It's phenomenal how quickly intellectual confusion begins to evaporate when we come to the one who is *the* truth. Some intellectuals are finding this today—certainly many students are as they question the theories and answers that many so-called thinkers present as truths. Review the problems surrounding modern man and the problems of people you know. Then ask yourself how the Lord Jesus speaks to these problems. Enter into the reality of this by faith yourself, and then communicate it to others.

5 FAITH NEEDS AN OBJECT

"Is Christianity credible?" Even some persons who personally believe may wonder how well Christianity could hold up under vigorous investigation. Although they have faith, and they're hanging on to it, they think that the little Sunday school boy may have been correct when he defined faith as "believing something you know isn't really true."

Enemies of Christianity are edgy about the question because if it were to turn out that Christianity is credible, it would have enormous implications for their personal lives.

For many, the problem of the credibility of Christianity has to do with the fact that Christianity requires an element of faith. The word *faith* makes a lot of people nervous, particularly thinking people, and the reason is that *faith* in our society is a foggy, misunderstood word.

An airplane comes in safely after having developed engine trouble and the passengers ask the pilot, "How did you do it?" He says, "Well, we came in by faith," and everybody gets a warm, glowy feeling inside. They're not quite sure what he means, but faith is so wonderful, and they feel great. Or you're about to flunk out of school and somebody slaps you on the back and says, "That's all right, just have faith." Used this way, the word *faith* really doesn't mean a thing. More thoughtful people see little meaning in that usage, so they begin to wonder whether faith is not essentially superstition.

Other people say to those who have a personal relationship with Jesus Christ, "I wish I had your faith—it's wonderful—but I just can't believe." Some people do have real problems in believing, but what most people mean when they say they can't believe is, "I've got a little bit too much upstairs, and I can't be quite that naive. It must be wonderful to be that simpleminded, and I wish I could be, but I'm not."

A man sat in the park reading a paperback book, and as he read each page he ripped it out, tore it up in little pieces, and scattered them around the bench. He did this with page after page until a policeman observing him came up and said, "Sir, apart from the fact that you're littering, I wonder if you would mind telling me why, after you read each page, you tear it out and scatter it on the ground?" The fellow brightened and said, "Sure, it's to keep the elephants away."

"To keep the elephants away? I don't see any elephants."

The fellow responded, "Pretty effective, isn't it?"

To some people there is no more cause and effect relationship between faith and reality than in the "keep-the-elephants-away" concept, and so they don't see how a thinking person can have a vital personal faith in Jesus Christ.

Faith and Its Object

To intelligently discuss faith, we must keep three observations in mind. The first is that *faith is no more valid than the object in which it is placed*, whether that object is a person or a thing. If the object of our faith is valid, we have valid faith. If the object of our faith is invalid, we have nothing more than superstition.

A witch doctor in a primitive culture prepares a brew that he gives to a desperately anxious father whose little daughter is seriously ill with a high fever. The father takes the potion to his daughter because he has intense faith and belief. He is very sincere, but his sincerity doesn't save the life of his daughter if the witch doctor's potion happens to be poisonous. In this case the father's faith amounts to nothing more than superstition, since the object of his faith is invalid.

Don't Believe Everything

The second observation is that believing something false doesn't make it true, and failing to believe something true, no matter how distasteful, doesn't make it false.

To illustrate the point that believing something doesn't make it true, a little old lady rented a room to a seemingly nice college student. She continued to think he was fine and upstanding until she came home one day and found the whole house cleaned out—nothing but the curtain rods left. She told the police when they came around to investigate, "He was such a nice boy; he even had YMCA on his towel." She believed implicitly in the young man, but that didn't save her possessions!

The Starving Millionaire

On the other hand, failing to believe something doesn't erase truth.

A poverty-stricken recluse in Texas, one of those people with cats running all over the place and newspapers stuffed everywhere, was informed that he had inherited a million dollars from a relative in England whom he didn't even realize existed. It was a fact—the recluse was heir to a million dollars, but tragically he didn't believe it and died a starving old man. His unbelief robbed him of the enjoyment of his wealth.

Faith enables us to enter into the reality of that which is already true, but it doesn't create truth out of something which is not objectively true already. Nor does lack of faith erase truth; what's true is true, and our opinion of the truth doesn't change the fact of it one bit. There's nothing spooky about the word *faith*; it simply means trust in what is true.

Everyone Uses Faith

The third observation is that every one of us exercises faith each day we live. There's a strange notion going around in some circles that faith is something reserved for a small group of peculiar people—you know, you either have it or you don't. It's wonderful if you have it, but if you don't have it—well, that's just too bad. But the fact is that faith is *not* something reserved for a particular type of emotionally constructed person.

When we go to a restaurant we eat food that we didn't see prepared (if we did see it prepared, we might not eat it!). We ate the food in blind faith, and just how blind we may never know unless we go behind the scenes.

We all exercise *reasonable* faith every day. We usually don't drop like flies from ptomaine poisoning in our favorite restaurant. But we did exercise faith in eating there.

The student who enrolls in a college exercises faith in that college; he assumes that after completing a certain series of course requirements he will be awarded a degree. If he didn't believe that, he would transfer to the most odious rival possible. If he thought that this year the institution would suddenly say, "Well, we don't want to be conformists, so this year we're not going to award any degrees," he would change schools immediately. People exercise *faith* in the college of their choice!

When I first learned that I had a pulmonic condition and that it possibly could be corrected, I read everything about pulmonic ailments that I could get my hands on. I even went down to the library and read the medical journals on the subject. I remember one scholarly, eight-page article which ended, "We can therefore conclude, in the light of data thus far, that there are basically three results of heart surgery: one, marked improvement; two, no improvement; three, death." Well, I thought to myself, that was tremendously profound! I had that suspicion myself before I read the article, but it was wonderful to have it confirmed by scientific data!

I got all the information I could about heart surgery. I checked out the surgeon's record and talked to some people who had had this kind of surgery. I became convinced that the thing for me to do would be to undergo heart surgery, but I still had to exercise faith. My reason took me up to a certain point, but beyond that I had to have faith. Although I had all the information I could get my hands on, if that was all the farther I had gone, I would still have that heart condition today. The doctor told me, "If you continue without surgery, in ten to fifteen years your heart will probably enlarge so much that it will collapse."

Faith Beyond Reason

Fortunately, my faith went beyond my reason. I committed my life to that surgeon. I exercised reasonable faith, since all the data pointed in that direction. In many experiences of life, faith goes beyond reason.

This is the case in Christianity. Faith goes *beyond* reason but not *against* reason. There are many things we may not fully understand, but this does not prevent us from entering into the reality of them.

Is Christianity credible? Yes. Christianity is the most credible experience and life system and key to meaning in the universe. Some questions are unanswered, to be sure, but when we exercise faith in Jesus Christ, we find from both the historical and experiential data that He is a worthy object of our faith. As we come to Him we are never disappointed.

Science and Faith

Even the scientific method itself, which we all recognize to be one of the most objective mechanisms by which we come to the experience of reality, ultimately rests upon faith. Three unproven axioms must be accepted by faith before we can proceed with the scientific method: first, the continuity of yesterday, today, and tomorrow; second, the reliability of our sense perceptions; and third, the orderliness of the universe. We accept these by faith in order to make scientific progress. If we didn't believe these assumptions, there would be no basis for the scientific method. Even the most objective method of determining reality has within it an element of faith. Faith is really nothing to be afraid of!

The real question is not whether one person has faith and another person doesn't; the real question is whether the object of our faith is worth trusting. When we're discussing the question "Is Christianity credible?", we recognize that the object of one's Christian faith is Jesus Christ; so the question we must ask ourselves is, "Is Jesus Christ a valid object for my faith? Is He a trustworthy person? Is He someone to whom I can commit myself with confidence?" In order to answer it we must examine two basic lines of evidence: external and internal.

6 IS THE OBJECT VALID?

The external evidence about Jesus Christ is totally outside our own personal experience because it deals with the solid facts of history. There is a large body of historical facts about Jesus Christ, and if we're honest in our approach we must forthrightly face up to them. Among these sources are the four Gospels in the New Testament: Matthew, Mark, Luke, and John.

Regardless of our point of view with reference to the divine inspiration of these particular documents, we must recognize that they are historical documents which have been well-validated. Sir William Ramsay, the famous nineteenth-century British archaeologist, stated that Luke was one of the most accurate historians of his time. Luke was the physician who wrote the Gospel of Luke. The four Gospel accounts are documentary biographies of Jesus Christ that present a whole body of information about this unique person. They are remarkable documents when we come to grips with them, for even a superficial reading of them tells us with striking force that *Jesus Christ literally claimed to be God in human form.*

I think sometimes the electricity of this claim escapes us in the twentieth century.

If I were to stand here and say, "Ladies and gentlemen, do you want to know what God is like? Take a look," it would be frighteningly bad, actually blasphemous. If you thought I was serious, you would immediately excuse yourself to call the men with the white coats before I started getting violent.

Is God Jesus Christ?

Jesus Christ was in earnest when he identified Himself as the living God. There's no mistaking His claim to deity, because as we know from reading the four Gospels this was the very claim that led to His crucifixion. He was killed because He claimed to be God. His enemies said, "We have a law, and by it this man ought to die." They referred to the law against blasphemy—a mere man making himself into God—and so Jesus Christ was crucified.

One instance of His claim to deity appears in the Gospel of John. Jesus said to the Jews,"I and my Father are one" (John 10:30). Then they took up stones to stone him (v. 31). Jesus replied, "I have shown you many good works from my Father; for which of these works do you stone me?"

(v. 32). The Jews answered, "We stone you for no good work, but for blasphemy, because you, being a man, make yourself to be God" (v. 33).

Later Philip, one of the disciples, said to Him, "Lord, show us the Father, and we shall be satisfied" (John 14:8). Jesus turned to Philip and in very remarkable words said to him, "Have I been with you so long and yet you do not know me, Philip? He who has seen me has seen the Father" (John 14:9). It is a claim that all of must face sooner or later.

Liar?

The staggering claims of Jesus have only four possible explanations. One is that He was a liar— that He knew He was not God, but deliberately deceived people in an attempt to give weight to His particular brand of religious teaching. To postulate that Jesus was a liar is shocking right on the surface, and not many people hold to this point of view, since even those who deny that Jesus was God usually acknowledge that He was a great moral philosopher and teacher. A stark inconsistency exists in this position. If Jesus was wrong on the most crucial point of His teaching, He could hardly be considered a great teacher of any kind. The fact is that it's simply incredible that the propounder of the most widely acclaimed ethical system in the world could have been a deliberate liar.

Megalomania?

A second possibility is that Jesus was a lunatic. Again, that's a bald statement, but we do need to recognize that some people say that Jesus was sincere but had lost contact with reality—sort of like people today who think they're Napoleon or George Washington or, in fact, Jesus Christ. Mental institutions have people who suffer from this particular mental disturbance, but we know today what the symptoms of paranoia and megalomania are, and as we compare the life of Jesus with what we know the clinical symptoms of these disturbances to be, we find no comparison. On the contrary, Jesus Christ manifested symptoms and characteristics of sublime sanity and dignity. He was tremendously poised in the midst of enormous pressure. For example, at the time of His death He was the quintessence of poise and composure. Even His enemies were astonished. Pontius Pilate, the hardened Roman governor who held Christ's earthly life in his hands, couldn't understand the composure of this man in crisis.

Legend?

A third possibility is that Jesus never made these claims—that it's a legend. What actually happened, according to this theory, is that His enthusiastic followers in the third and fourth centuries got carried away and attributed words to Him that He would be shocked to hear and would immediately disown if He were on earth today. According to this theory, the whole story developed over a period of time, since people tend to legendize everybody and everything significant.

This point of view was widely held in the early twentieth century, but a wealth of archaeological discoveries have demonstrated conclusively that the Gospels and much of the remainder of the New Testament were written not in the third and fourth centuries, as had previously been supposed, but rather within the lifetimes of the very contemporaries of Jesus. According to the late William F. Albright, one of the world's leading archaeologists, some of Paul's epistles could easily have been written as early as 50 A.D., and there is no reason to believe that any book in the New Testament was written later than 70 A.D. As a result the time lag necessary for this elaborate kind of legend to develop just wasn't there. It would be as absolutely fantastic as somebody in our time writing a book about the late President Franklin Delano Roosevelt and saying that he claimed to be God, claimed to forgive people's sins, claimed that he would rise from the dead, and in fact did rise from the dead.

Not everyone admired President Roosevelt, but I've never heard him accused of these kind of claims. The whole thing would be so wild that it would never get off the ground, because there are too many people around who knew Roosevelt and knew that he never made such claims.

We must never delude ourselves into thinking that the people who lived during New Testament times were naive, sheepish people who believed everything they heard. Actually some people were bitterly antagonistic toward Jesus and Christianity at that time, even to the point of committing murder (just as in our time). Some people in the first century would have given anything to see

Christianity strangled in its cradle, but the truth of Jesus Christ and His claims prevailed against even bitter opposition.

We Must Choose

Jesus Christ, then, in terms of His claim to deity, was either a liar, a legend, a lunatic, or the truth. These are the only four possibilities. I have had eager students come roaring up to me suggesting possibility number five, but invariably this "fifth possibility" is just a slight variation on one of the other four. Therefore, if we say that Christ is not the truth, we are automatically affirming one of the other three positions. If we make such a claim we need to ask ourselves, "What evidence can we produce to confirm this particular point of view, evidence which would persuade a truly thoughtful person?"

The claim of Jesus Christ is quite clear: it is a piece of history we must grapple with and explain in one way or another.

7 CHRIST'S CREDENTIALS

Since talk is cheap, the heart of the issue about Christ's claim to deity is *the credentials He presents* in order to substantiate His claim. If *I* were to make this claim to deity I'm sure it wouldn't take you very long to disprove it, and I suspect that if *you* were to make the claim it wouldn't take me very long to disprove yours either! But the astounding thing is that it is not easy to disprove His claim to deity, since He provided the credentials to substantiate His claim and to demonstrate that He spoke the truth.

For one thing, Christ lived a life of such utter moral perfection that even His enemies were unable to challenge Him on this point. Most of us would hesitate to expose ourselves completely to even our closest friends, to challenge them to find anything wrong with us. But Jesus Christ said to His enemies, "Which of you can convict me of sin?" And none of them could. If you read through the four Gospels you'll find that all of His enemies, including Pilate, the Roman governor, said in effect, "We agree. This man has never done anything wrong. He lived a life of absolute moral perfection."

The Authority of God

Jesus demonstrated that He had the authority of God over the physical elements of the universe— He healed people, He raised people from the dead, He controlled the winds and the waves, and He did many other supernatural acts. But the supreme test was His prediction made five times during the course of His earthly life that He was going to die but would rise from the dead three days later. Now that's a test.

The Resurrection of Christ

This is what Jesus Christ predicted, and the record that we have declares that Jesus rose bodily from the dead. His empty tomb is the universal symbol of Christianity, and inspires the celebration of Easter every year. The fact of His resurrection is what revolutionized that band of Christian disciples who were so frightened when Jesus was arrested that one of them denied he ever knew Jesus!

This is what changed the disciples into roaring lions, so that fifty days later Peter stood up and preached to two thousand people right in Jerusalem, the very place where he had denied Jesus. Peter had the newfound courage to say, "This same Jesus, whom you crucified, God has raised from the dead, whereby we have become eyewitnesses."

If the resurrection didn't happen and the record of it is a fable, we've simply got to explain it away in one way or another, and this is a remarkably difficult thing to do. The resurrection has been called the best-attested fact of ancient history.

One alternative theory has been advanced which, on the surface, seems rather plausible in explaining away the resurrection, but it is inadequate.

The Hallucination Theory

I was in college when I first heard about the hallucination theory, and for the moment it sounded very plausible to me—in fact, I didn't know why I hadn't thought of it myself. The hallucination theory says that Christ's followers just sort of talked themselves into believing Christ's resurrection. You know, they thought about it and thought about it and pretty soon they persuaded themselves that the whole thing had happened. Then they began to persuade other people, and pretty soon the whole thing grew into a widely accepted view. However, to have a hallucination, we must so intensely want to believe something that we ruminate on it, think about it, project it, and attach a reality out there, until finally we begin to move in that direction. But this first and absolute requirement, the intense desire to believe the resurrection, was strikingly absent from the record of the life of the disciples.

Take Mary, for instance. We have the record in each of the four Gospels, and in greatest detail in the twentieth chapter of John's Gospel, that on Sunday morning she came to the tomb with spices for entombment. Why did she have these spices? Not because she was expecting to see Jesus Christ rise from the dead, but because she wanted to anoint the dead body. So much was she *not* expecting to see Christ alive from the dead that when He spoke to her, she failed to recognize Him and mistook Him for the gardener. She asked, "Sir, where have they lain him?" She didn't get the message, didn't recognize Jesus until He addressed her by name.

When the women who had been at the tomb heard the message of resurrection from the angels, they ran to tell the eleven disciples, but the men accused the women of dreaming up fairy tales (Luke 24:1-11). Later, when Jesus appeared to the disciples in Jerusalem, they were so surprised that they thought they were seeing a ghost, and Jesus had to invite them to actually reach out and touch Him (Luke 24:36-40). This hardly lends weight to the hallucination theory!

Doubting Thomas

The classic example of unbelief was, of course, "doubting Thomas," whom we still refer to in this way. We have the record of his experience in John's Gospel. Because he had not been with the disciples the first time Jesus appeared, Thomas said, "Unless I see in his hands the print of the nails, and place my finger in the mark of the nails, and place my hand in his side, I will not believe" (John 24:25). Thomas wasn't about to have a hallucination! Remember how Jesus later met with Thomas and Thomas cried out, "My Lord and my God!" On the basis of this encounter with Jesus, Thomas became convinced against his will, so to speak, that Jesus Christ had risen from the dead. The actual, literal resurrection of Christ is truly the only event that adequately explains the history of the first century.

The Modern-day Thomas

A British lawyer by the name of Frank Morison was a modern-day Thomas. Morison was convinced that Christianity was nothing but a tissue of fabric, fable, and superstition. He correctly realized that the foundation-stone of Christianity was the resurrection of Christ, and he felt that if he could show conclusively that the resurrection was a fraud and a figment of the first-century imagination, he would once-and-for-all rid the world of Christianity, thereby doing it a great favor. As a lawyer, he felt he had the critical apparatus to rigidly evaluate evidence, throwing out anything that didn't meet the criteria that are necessary for evidence to be introduced into a court of law. So he set out to prove that the resurrection never happened.

When Morison's book was finally published, the first chapter had a curious title: "The Book

That Refused to Be Written." In this chapter
Morison described how he became persuaded
against his will that the resurrection had taken
place. By examining the evidence, Morison had to
acknowledge that the resurrection of Jesus Christ
was one of the greatest facts of world history.
Morison's book is titled *Who Moved the Stone?* and
is published by Zondervan Publishing House.

Knowing Christ Personally

The second avenue of evidence about the reality
of Christ's claim to deity has to do with contempo-
rary experiences of knowing Christ—the *personal*
verification of historical facts. If Jesus Christ is
who He claims to be, then He can and will do in
our lives today all the things He promised to do.
The real dynamic of Christianity is that Jesus
Christ is alive today, one with whom we can communicate and who will respond to us. We can
know Him in our personal experience.

We can, in the laboratory of life, validate the
hypothesis that Jesus Christ is, as He claimed, the
Son of God and the Savior of the world. We must
meet Jesus Christ on His conditions, that is, on
the basis of His substitutionary death and His
resurrection. Then we will find that He further
validates His claim by giving us inner peace and
directing our lives into God's purpose for history.

He gives new moral power and frees us from
the slavery to our sinful selves. He quenches our
spiritual hunger and thirst, relief that comes
from knowing the true and living God. He for-
gives our sins and cleanses us from guilt.

Modern Conversion Data

The interesting thing is that we have actual clinical data in the twentieth century by which we can come to grips with this issue. Many people from every conceivable background have had their lives transformed by Jesus Christ. It is not only (as some people think) those who have been raised in Christian homes who become Christians. People who have had little or no contact with Christianity have discovered Him to be the answer to the riddle of life and have had their views transformed by Him. Their experiences cannot be explained on a Pavlovian dog basis. (Pavlov fed dogs and rang a bell at the same time, and the dogs learned to salivate. Eventually, when he rang the bell and didn't feed them, they still salivated, with the reaction occurring from the psychological association.) There are those who suggest that this is the way all Christian experience is—you condition people in a Christian environment, and they become Christians.

But the explanation is not quite that simple, since many people become Christians despite no religious background. Whether you talk to a person who had no contact with Jesus Christ before becoming a Christian, or to a person who was raised in a Christian environment, both acknowledge that Jesus Christ became personal to them through that vital step of commitment. Both of them testify to the fact that the transformation that took place in their lives happened through a personal encounter with Jesus Christ.

I can think of a number of students (as well as

nonstudents) who fit into this category. I'm thinking of a fellow from SMU in Dallas who had done
everything in the book. You name it, he had been
involved in it. Finally he came to realize that
though he was a very sophisticated, handsome,
capable, and talented young man who made lots
of money in commercials, he was headed for a
dead end. He had observed that a couple of
Christians seemed to know what life was all
about. He got to talking with them. Then he committed his life to Jesus Christ and was revolutionized. His friends on the campus couldn't believe
that he was the same man, so great was his impact
on them.

Christianity Without Christ

On the other hand, I can think of a girl who had
been raised in a Christian environment. She
could give you all the answers, recite the cate-
chism, sing the hymns, quote Bible verses, and all
the rest, but Christianity didn't mean a thing to
her. Finally she too came to realize that, even
though she had taken Communion as a church
member, she was not a Christian. Eventually she
came to the place of personal commitment to
Christ and experienced the same life-transform-
ing revolution that takes place when anyone
comes to Christ.

So there is present-day data that we can observe. We can speak to people who have had the
experience of coming to know Christ personally,
and we can observe them, thereby validating
Christ's claim to deity by the results we see. This

up-to-date personal data buttresses the objective historical facts, and together these two lines of evidence provide overwhelming proof of the truthfulness of Christ's claim to deity.

8 HOW REAL IS HEAVEN?

When I was living in Dallas, Texas, a salesman of book classics of the Western world visited me. After his sales talk, in which he said I couldn't live without the books and we would deprive our children for life if we didn't purchase them, he told me I had to buy that night, since the offer expired in three minutes. I said, "Thank you very much, but good-bye. It's been nice to know you, but I don't appreciate that kind of approach."

But this man was very clever. He called back the next morning, saying, "I should have known better. You didn't have a chance to talk to your wife, so the offer has been extended." Well, in the end we bought a set of his books, and I vowed I was going to get my money's worth or die in the attempt. In retrospect I think the latter may be more true than the former!

In any case I ended up leafing through the *Syntopicon*, edited by Mortimer J. Adler. It's a very impressive and useful set of books, basically a dictionary of ideas plus an index of all the great thinkers of the Western world. The overview of the book pointed out that more space is devoted to the idea of God than any of the other 101 ideas in the *Syntopicon*, and more authors are quoted on this particular subject than on any other.

An interesting observation followed: "The reason for this is obvious: whether one is a believer or an unbeliever, more hangs on life and eternal destiny, on the whole question of God and the conclusion to which one comes with reference to this than on any other question of human existence."

I thought this was a striking comment, especially since it came from a secular commentary. How we deal with the concept of God is one of the most important matters in all of human experience. The implications of our decision concerning God and our relationship with Him are extremely far-reaching. The question of certainty of life after death is a crucial issue.

The Question of Heaven

In considering this issue, we first need to devote our attention to heaven itself. Many people say, "Heaven is everything that we experience here on earth." From my own viewpoint, that would be a rather dismal prospect! If heaven consisted only of life's happiest moments, it still would be a rather grim experience for many people. If we consider only human speculation, we fall prey to all kinds of ideas people have about heaven.

Herbert Spencer, the agnostic philosopher, observed that a bird has never been known to fly out into space; therefore, reasoned Spencer, it is obvious that the finite can never penetrate the infinite, and so even if God exists man can never know Him personally or anything about His existence.

Spencer was right when he observed that birds never fly out into space, but he missed the possibility that God, the infinite Creator, could penetrate our finiteness—that God Himself could take the initiative and come into human experience, thereby revealing to us what He is like and what heaven is like. This is exactly what God has done. This is the central thesis of Christianity—that God has penetrated human history in the person of Jesus Christ, thereby communicating to us authoritative information about these questions and ending the hopeless confusion that results from human-based speculations.

What Jesus Said About Heaven

Jesus Christ claims to be the revelation of God in human personality. When someone asks, "What is God like?" we can respond, "What is Jesus Christ like?" Jesus was very explicit about the reality of life after death, about the fact of heaven, and about believers being in heaven and knowing God personally.

We read some of the most comforting words of Jesus in John's Gospel: "Let not your hearts be troubled; believe in God, believe also in me. In my Father's house are many rooms; if it were not so, would I have told you that I go to prepare a place for you? And when I go and prepare a place for you, I will come again and will take you to myself, that where I am you may be also" (14:1-3).

John, who was one of Jesus' closest disciples, later wrote some very comforting words, speaking of heaven and of God: "He will dwell with them. . . . He will wipe away every tear from their eyes, and death shall be no more, neither shall there be mourning nor crying nor pain anymore, for the former things have passed away" (Rev. 21:3, 4).

It is clear from the words of Jesus Christ, as well as from other New Testament Scriptures, that heaven is a reality even though we don't yet know all about heaven. Many people have speculated about heaven, giving dimensions, as well as other fantasized ideas. Each person is entitled to his speculation, but we have to be careful not to attach Biblical authority to it.

We don't know where heaven is geographically, but we do know that heaven is where God is. We also know that heaven will be the most wonderful place we can imagine, the place to which everyone who really trusts in God looks forward to going.

A popular misconception about heaven that we often see in cartoons and hear people talk about is that of sitting on a cloud and strumming a harp—a boring prospect. Heaven will be the most dynamic, expanding experience we can imagine. It's a place we look forward to, not only for rest, but for stimulating activity as well as worshiping God.

Jesus referred to heaven as paradise. Perhaps the most famous of His statements about heaven was made while He was on the cross. One of the two thieves on the crosses nearby slandered Jesus to the effect, "If He's so great, why doesn't He do something about all this?" The other thief, of a more humble strain, realized that Jesus was suffering innocently and said to the other thief, "We are receiving the due reward of our deeds; but this man has done nothing wrong" (Luke 23:41). Then he appealed to Jesus Christ to forgive him. Jesus turned to him in words that must have electrified the thief: "Today you will be with me in paradise" (Luke 23:43). That thief had absolute certainty that when death came he would be in the presence of God.

Actually, we can be as sure as the thief that when death comes we can be in the presence of God in paradise. Jesus said, "I give to my sheep eternal life, and they will never perish, neither shall any man pluck them out of my hand" (John 10:28). Jesus states clearly that every person who trusts Him as Savior can be sure of eternal life.

Eternal Existence for Everyone

Jesus also made it clear that every human being has eternal existence. Those who will be in heaven in direct and vital relationship with the living God through Jesus Christ are spoken of as having eternal life. Those who will be eternally separat-

ed from God because of their rebellion and refus-
al to accept what God has done for them in Jesus
Christ are spoken of as being in eternal punishment. "And they will go away into eternal punishment, but the righteous into eternal life" (Matt.
25:46). Every human being will exist forever.
Eternal life, as Jesus used the term, refers to the
future of those who enter into a relationship of
salvation with Him. They are assured of being in
the presence of God for all eternity.

Another Biblical evidence of the hereafter
comes from the First Epistle of John where we
read, "These things have I written unto you who
believe in the name of the Son of God, that you
may know that you have eternal life" (5:13). This
is not something that we'll discover at the end of
life, breathlessly hoping that we've made it, but
rather we can be absolutely certain right now if
we're willing to believe what Jesus Christ promised.

The Fact of Christ's Death

What is the basis for certainty of being in heaven
after life on this earth is over? It is the fact that
Jesus died. Even superficial reading of the New
Testament makes it clear that Jesus Christ had a
mission when He came into human history.

Christ was born to die," playwright Dorothy L.
Sayers concisely stated. Jesus said He came into
human history in order to give His life, so that
men and women could be reconciled to God.
"The Son of man came not to be served, but to
serve, and to give his life a ransom for many"

(Mark 10:45). Was Christ's mission successful? Yes. To as many as receive Him, Christ gives eternal life which starts right now and continues on into heaven forever. The believing is up to you.

9 CAN WE BE SURE OF HEAVEN?

When God's perfect creatures exercised their freedom of choice and rebelled against Him, He couldn't just brush the sins aside and say, "We'll forget the whole thing and everything will be fine; everybody can come into heaven." God couldn't do that and still be the moral upholder of the universe. You and I would want to impeach a judge who failed to sentence a son who was found guilty of a crime. As the one who upholds the law of the land, this judge cannot change the law or the punishment for the benefit of his son. He must maintain justice.

Although God's infinite holiness makes it impossible for Him to overlook sin, God loves us. He doesn't want to execute judgment upon us. But how can He manifest His love to us and at the same time uphold His holiness and righteousness? God Himself, in the person of His son Jesus Christ, voluntarily took the sentence of judgment which belonged to you and me by dying on the cross. Now His justice is fully satisfied and He can freely offer us reconciliation, forgiveness, and assurance of life after death.

God's Part

There's a sad but true story of two men who went to university together in Australia. One ultimately became a banker, and the other a lawyer and later a judge. Both of the men had brilliant careers, but after about twenty years the banker was charged with embezzling several million dollars. The case came up before the judge who was the college friend of the banker. There was a great deal of speculation in the press as to what would happen. If the banker was found guilty, what would this judge do? Because the defendant was his friend, would he be lenient in sentencing? Or would he, for fear of criticism, be overly tough?

The case was tried with a packed courtroom, and finally a guilty verdict was brought in. When the time came for sentencing, the people were shocked when the judge stood and read the maximum sentence which could be imposed—one hundred thousand dollars.

Then the spectators saw the judge stand, walk around the bench, take off his robe, and put his arm around his friend and say, "I have sold my house and every one of my investments, and I will pay this debt for you." The judge risked bankruptcy in order to pay the debt which was necessary if justice was to be carried out. At the same time, he showed his love for his friend.

This is only a faint illustration of what God has done for us in Jesus Christ. This is the basis on which we can be sure of forgiveness of sin and of eternal life in God's presence in heaven.

Our Part

But there is another aspect to assuring our presence in heaven, and that is faith. That's our part. To be personally sure of being in heaven with God for all eternity, we must exercise personal faith in Jesus Christ as our own Savior and Lord. Faith simply allows us to experience that which is *already true*. Faith enables us to experience *the reality that already is*. The fact that Jesus Christ died and rose again makes it *possible* for every one of us to be forgiven and reconciled, but to personally experience this relationship with the living God we *must exercise faith* in the Lord Jesus Christ as our personal Savior.

We're all tremendously grateful to Dr. Jonas Salk and Dr. Albert Sabin for their tremendous research in order to immunize us against polio. But the fact that polio protection is available doesn't mean a thing to you or me unless we have personally taken the vaccine.

That's exactly the way it is with reference to the death of Jesus Christ and the question of assurance of heaven. Christ died for us, so it is *possible* for us to have certainty, but this possibility doesn't mean a thing unless we have personally

entered into a relationship with Jesus Christ
Himself.

Not by Good Works

Many people have the mistaken idea that our assurance of eternal life and of heaven is somehow
based on what we do for God—the kind of life we
live and the good works we perform. They feel
that if somehow our good works can outweigh
our bad works, there's a good chance we might
make it into heaven. The fact of the matter is that
if our assurance of heaven is based on the works
that you or I do, there is really no chance at all.
How do you or I ever know when we've done
enough good works to qualify for the presence of
God? It's an impossibility. "All have sinned and
come short of the glory of God" (Rom. 3:23).

Deep inside we all know we've missed God's
standard of absolute perfection—we've been corrupt in thought and action and word. It is therefore impossible for us to come into the presence
of God and to be related to Him on the basis of
the life we've lived. It is not a question of *what we
do for God*, but of *what God has done for us*.

If salvation were based on works, heaven
would be an intolerably proud society. If eternal
life were based on what we did, we know well
enough that we would be tooting our horns and
looking down our noses at those who didn't quite
make it. Salvation on this basis would be a contra-
diction of terms: heaven would be hell with that
kind of attitude dominating.

Paul the Apostle was explicit on this point: "By

grace you have been saved through faith, and this is not your own doing; it is the gift of God—not because of works, lest any man should boast" (Eph. 2:8, 9). Works are not the basis on which any of us can be sure of our relationship to God and our place in heaven. If it were, there would be no hope for any of us. Instead, our hope is in what God has done for us.

Nicodemus was a cultured man, a leader among the Jews, a lawyer, and a university graduate, but he didn't understand this truth at first. Nicodemus was trying to figure out who Jesus was, so he said, "Rabbi, we know you are a teacher come from God, for no one can do these signs that you do unless God is with him" (John 3:2).

Jesus replied, "Unless one is born anew, he cannot see the kingdom of God" (John 3:3). Nicodemus was a little startled by this statement, since he took it in the physical sense. He didn't quite understand that. "How can a man be born again when he is old?" He couldn't figure out how one could go through this whole process of physical birth again. Jesus said to him, "That which is born of the flesh is flesh and that which is born of the Spirit is spirit. Do not marvel that I said to you 'you must be born anew'" (John 3:7).

We need to be born *spiritually* if we are to see the kingdom of God. Jesus continued by pointing out to Nicodemus that though every human being has *physical* life by virtue of being born into this world, we don't have *spiritual* life because of this physical birth. As a matter of fact, every human being is born spiritually dead because of our separation from God. The only way we can be sure of entering the kingdom of God is to have a *spiritual birth*, to be born again as Jesus Christ described it to Nicodemus. It's not something that happens to us naturally, but something that happens to us when we make a definite personal transaction with Jesus Christ. Then we are born into *His* family—we become *His* children and we qualify to become citizens of *His* heaven, the kingdom of God.

It's Not How We Feel

Eternal life is not based on our feelings. Some people say, "Well, I feel like I'm a Christian." And there are others who say, "I don't feel like I'm a Christian." When we wake up in the morning with a headache, the toast is burned, and the scrambled eggs are sort of sour, we don't feel like much of anything. Our assurance of salvation could be blown to bits if it's based on personal feelings.

If we are to be sure of our relationship with God, if we are to be sure of our destiny in heaven, our assurance cannot rest on how we feel, but rather on God's promise of personal relationship through Christ. Let's say I've had sixteen meetings in three days, and students have been talking to me until 4 in the morning, and somebody comes to me and says, "Do you feel married?" I would have to say I don't feel like much of anything at that point except flopping somewhere. If somebody says to me, "Do you know you're married?" I say, "Sure, I know I'm married." I don't feel anything except bone-weariness at that point, but I know I'm married because the certainty of my marriage relationship hinges on the fact that at a particular time and place I committed myself to my wife and she to me—we established a permanent relationship. Our feelings come and go, but the *abiding relationship* is what counts in marriage as well as in salvation.

You may have heard the old proverb of Mr. Fact, Mr. Faith, and Mr. Feeling. Mr. Fact, Mr. Faith, and Mr. Feeling were walking along a very narrow wall. As long as Mr. Faith kept his eye on Mr. Fact, Mr. Feeling followed right along and they made beautiful progress. But every time Mr. Faith turned around and looked at Mr. Feeling, they almost fell off, because they were so paralyzed with fear. The moral of the story is that our feelings will follow our faith in the facts. Certainty of salvation rests in the fact of what God has done for us in Jesus Christ and the fact of our personal commitment to Jesus Christ. If our faith lies in these facts, we find our feelings following along without difficulty.

No Room for Arrogance

When we have the certainty that should death come to us tonight we would be in the presence of God, this does not mean we are arrogant. Some people are disturbed that anyone should have the audacity to say, "I'm sure I am related to the living God and have eternal life." They misunderstand this person as saying, "I'm a hotshot, and if you were as good a hotshot as I am, you could have this same certainty."

Assurance of salvation is not based on pride in any way, shape, or form, since our assurance has nothing to do with what *we* have done, but rather with what *God has done for us in Jesus Christ.* Basically, the person who says he knows he will be in heaven is simply taking God at His word. He is believing that God has spoken the truth, and he is claiming God's promise.

No Careless Attitudes

Being sure of our relationship to Jesus Christ and being certain of heaven does not mean that we can develop a careless attitude toward life and sin. I've had people say to me, "Well, if you're sure you have eternal life and will be in the presence of God, that means there's no incentive for you to live a good life. You could live as you please! That can't possibly be the way God works." This is an understandable misconception. It would perhaps seem on the surface that this criticism is true—that if a person is sure of his salvation he would live in sin and disobedience. In thinking of this, one vital overwhelming fact is overlooked: when a personal relationship with Jesus Christ is established, an internal revolution takes place within the life of the person who encounters Jesus Christ.

A New Creation

The Apostle Paul goes so far as to call this becoming a new creation. Our whole orientation toward life changes—what interested us before, no longer does. Spiritual realities that before didn't interest us in the least, suddenly become vitally interesting. We find that we have a greater sensitivity to sin and rebellion against God in our lives, and we begin to loathe sin.

Because we love Jesus Christ and recognize what He has done for us by giving His life in love, we find that we want to do nothing that will displease or hurt Him. When we become conscious of violating His law or of doing something wrong, it pains us and we immediately want reconciliation and forgiveness.

When a person encounters Jesus Christ as Savior and Lord, the whole relationship is changed, and the believer doesn't need a club of fear. Love is a much stronger incentive.

If a Christian sins after he has come into this relationship with Jesus Christ, it does not mean that he loses this relationship; rather, *the fellowship and communion within that relationship* have to be reestablished.

Again, think of marriage as an illustration. Being married is a one-time situation. We receive a person into our lives by committing ourselves to that person—a permanent marriage relationship. But suppose a year later we develop marital tensions. Somebody walks into our house and could cut the atmosphere with a knife. Something is wrong somewhere. But do we need to go out and get married again? No. What we need is to have our *fellowship and communion* restored. That will take place only when one or both parties (as the case may require) make confession and restoration. Then the air is cleared, forgiveness is granted, communication is restored, and communion and fellowship are reestablished. The relationship was always there, but the fellowship and communion were not.

It's Permanent

This is what happens when we come to the place of commitment to Jesus Christ as Savior and Lord and are concerned about doing His will. When we sin or disobey, we don't need to have the *relationship* reestablished, but we do need to confess our sins and ask for the forgiveness which Jesus Christ promises. Then fellowship and communion will be restored.

When we understand that the certainty of eternal life is based exclusively on the fact of our personal relationship with Jesus Christ as Savior and Lord, we can understand the inadequacy of certain so-called bases of assurance that some people are depending on. Heredity, for example, is one that some are leaning on. You ask them, "Will you be in heaven?" and they say, "Oh, yes, our family has been Christian for four generations!" or "I was born a Christian!" That's like saying to a person, "How long have you been married?" only to have him reply, "Oh, I was born married!" It's an impossibility. Salvation has to be established in personal, individual terms.

Others think that a particular ritual or a recognized church membership will guarantee their future in heaven. As a friend has observed, a

Christian will always go to church, but going to church no more makes a person a Christian or gives him assurance of heaven than going into a garage makes him an automobile. It just doesn't work that way! A Christian goes to church *not* as a means by which to be sure, but as an expression of that certainty.

It's Sure

Every one of us can be absolutely sure that we will be in heaven if we have personally committed ourselves to Jesus Christ in an act of faith. The way we can answer for ourselves the question, "Can I be sure of being in heaven?" is by answering the question, "Have I ever personally, specifically, and definitely invited Jesus Christ to come into my life as Savior and Lord?" If I have done that, then on the authority of what God Himself says in His Word I can be absolutely sure of heaven and of an eternity with Jesus Christ. This is the way to be sure of the eternal relationship of love which God offers in Jesus Christ.